HIKING

FOR THE CouchPotato™

A Guide for the Exercise-Challenged

Shelley Gillespie

Hiking for the Couch Potato: A Guide for the Exercise-Challenged

For information about this title, to order other books and/or electronic media, or for incentive or corporate orders, contact the publisher:

Venture Court Productions
P.O. Box 357
Maricopa, AZ 85139
info@FortheCouchPotato.com
orders@FortheCouchPotato.com

ISBN: 978-0-9829554-0-6 (soft cover)
      978-0-9829554-1-3 (e-book)

Printed in the United States of America

Cover design and illustrations by Kedrick Ridges
Interior design by 1106 Design
Photos by Shelley Gillespie

PRINTER INFORMATION
First Edition/First Printing

Dedicated to Roger, the inspiration and motivation for the Couch Potato becoming a hiker and this book becoming a reality.

ACKNOWLEDGMENTS

MUCH LIKE THOSE AT AWARDS CEREMONIES, I would like to thank everyone I've ever known who has brought me to this point in my life. That mentioned, there are certain people and groups that I'd like to single out for a little extra applause because they contributed to this book.

The winners are:

Michele, Ronda, Diane and Doran at 1106 Design, who have helped my manuscript become this book. Ronda is an especial gem, as she is endlessly patient and amazingly efficient.

Kedrick Ridges, whose talent provided the illustrations I'd always envisioned.

My "Computer God," Traek Malan, who worked to make everything work—at all hours of the day and night. (ungatech.com)

The many trails that I've experienced and, especially, the ones that are well-marked.

The friends who encouraged me, particularly Gina, Jackie, Phyllis, and Shawn.

My family, who believed in me.

Andrew, for his perseverance, expertise and moral support. (Patentbest.com)

And, most of all, Roger Gillespie, who inspired me to get moving, both in life and in writing.

TABLE OF CONTENTS

Hiking for the Couch Potato

ONCE UPON A TIME there was a person who preferred to read, curled up on the sofa with a good—or not-so-good—book. Due to a cold climate, a child to raise, an exhausting job, and other reasons and excuses, she was largely—and I do mean *largely*—sedentary.

In other words, she was a world-class sitter. The couch was molded to certain parts of her anatomy. Long evenings, and weekend hours, would be whiled away munching, reading, and stretched out on the couch. She personified the "Couch Potato"—"A person who spends much time sitting or lying down, usually watching television." (*Webster's II New College Dictionary*, 1995)

Then, something changed. Actually, a lot of things changed. The kids grew up, the single person found another single person and married, and they moved to a new climate. Suddenly, it was appealing to get out and see something of nature.

Armed with a camera, water, hiking socks, boots, hiking pole, and trail guides, the Couch Potato became a hiker. Not an easy transition, at first it took a lot of prodding and positive thinking. Gradually, it got easier. Finally, the Couch Potato realized that she was a hiker who really looked forward to outdoor encounters. Like birds and bees, flowers and trees, flora and fauna, and a lot of sunshine.

The world does look better out in the sunshine. With sun block at the ready, the vitamin D you get from the sun is good for you! Although your mama may have made vegetables and other good things—like exercise—seem difficult to take, you are now an adult. The great thing about hiking is that you get to make your own decisions!

So, do something for yourself! Try it—you might like it.

—The Author

CHAPTER 1

Not an Easy Beginning

THE COUCH POTATO was not instantly enthusiastic about beginning outdoor adventures. In urban areas, she had sprained her ankle—twice—and had visions of Hansel and Gretel getting lost in the forest or other misfortunes.

Remembering earlier camping experiences didn't help, either. On a camping event as a teenager assigned to KP (kitchen patrol), she had fallen in the stream while washing dishes. Wet, soggy and traveling without a change of clothes, she was embarrassed and cold. The boys' camp was nearby and they got to see her in her drenched state. This did not promote positive feelings about the great outdoors.

As a young girl in the scouts, she also remembered the time her troop was camped downwind from the latrine. "Fragrance" was too kind a word to describe the smell. "Stench" was perhaps more accurate. Not a pretty memory!

And, she was concerned about allergies. So, there were lots of excuses.

As she learned about hiking, one by one, her excuses went away. Fortunately, her guide was an experienced hiker who had hiked in very demanding situations and locations. The guide, better known as husband, was very matter of fact. You take precautions and prepare. You find places with well-marked trails so you don't get lost. You arrive at a place to hike. You get out and hike.

So, her fears allayed, her husband took her for a shopping excursion. Hey, shopping, who wouldn't like that as a beginning for a new adventure?

Perhaps it was shopping for the new hiking boots or poles that distracted her from how she would actually be using the purchases. (More on hiking equipment later.) Maybe it was just that the hiking trail sounded so interesting. Or, perhaps it was just that staying in the house was getting boring.

One day, the Couch Potato just went for a walk. Or so it seemed.

All of this proves that even the non-athletic among us can enjoy the brief visits to nature that hiking provides. Whether it be birds, butterflies, competitive races on a trail, or getting away from chores, hiking provides a change of place and pace for our hectic lives.

Why not just go walking? Well, that's good, too. Many studies show how important walking is to our health. For this Couch Potato, however, walking seemed less interesting than hiking. Walking seemed to imply flat surfaces and less interesting surroundings. Besides, hiking offered an excuse to put on those sharp hiking boots and grab some poles.

The Act of Hiking: Having "Attitude"

A hike, defined in *Webster's Dictionary* as "To go on an extended walk for pleasure or exercise," seemed an impossibility. Hike—for pleasure? These two concepts seemed mutually exclusive.

Hiking as a concept seemed *definitely* alien.

Basic exercise for most Couch Potatoes is to move the finger on the remote or, at worst, get up for a snack. Nimble fingers from working the remote are the most agile part of the Couch Potato species. But this can change!

Why Change?

Well, there are a number of reasons to change. Being a Couch Potato can get boring. By the time you've seen the same movie on one of the extended cable channels three or more times, you are probably tired of that. If you have memorized the movie and can recite the dialogue word-for-word, you probably should audition for some theatrical pursuit. (Which would also mean getting off the couch!)

Daytime broadcasting is not all that entertaining. (Apologies to the avid fans of soap operas. Briefly, the Couch Potato was one of those fans. By the time she realized that it took a very l-o-o-o-o-ng time for anything to *happen* on a soap, she was empowered to miss a few episodes.) Besides, that is what video recorders are for! Save your favorite episodes for an evening or rainy day.

If the spuds you've been nibbling are adhering to your middle and you have an unhealthy pallor, an outdoor excursion might be just the activity you need. More on this as you resolve to …

Get in Shape

Although most people don't care about our country's obesity epidemic, getting in shape is another matter. You will probably live longer if you remove yourself from the couch and go outside.

Calories? Who wants to count calories? The Couch Potato didn't particularly, but the fact is that you burn almost six times as many calories by hiking than by sitting still for one hour. Even walking at a slow two miles per hour burns more than twice as many calories as just sitting. And, why do we want to burn calories?

Well, 3,500 of those ugly things make a pound. Every pound we get rid of makes most of us healthier. (We exempt the minority of people who are the ideal weight for their height.) The Couch Potato knew for her weight that she'd need to be about six feet tall to be healthy. Assuredly, she is not six feet tall, nor her ideal weight, but she is healthier since she took up hiking. And after hiking, no, she does not indulge in an apple pie orgy, tempting as that may be, to reward herself for hiking. That would cancel out the calories she burned in a one-hour hike. (See Appendix II for URL for calorie burning activities chart.)

There are no guarantees in life, but hiking is one way to get healthier. Plus, we can visit the **Great Outdoors.**

But, frankly, is it really the *Great* Outdoors?

Well, it depends. If you go walking with car fumes and busy traffic to accompany you, then, no, the outdoors isn't so great. However, a quiet hike on a trail with the prospect of seeing a memorable view or a small creature is far superior.

Views vary, depending on where you hike. So, there are no assurances about picturesque views.

However, there are other compensations.

Clothes, for example. You can enjoy the clothes that are practical for hiking. Since hikers don't have a "uniform" the way people who participate in organized sports do, the new hiker should choose clothes that make hiking fun and have lots of pockets to store "indispensable" items. Getting a "look" for your hiking excursion can definitely provide an excuse to hit the stores. Shopping is a great transition from being a Couch Potato to being a hiker.

When you hike, you make it possible for clothes to fit better. You might even drop a size! Exercise—who wants to exercise? But, movement is everything! If you are out seeing the world and moving about, you are getting exercise.

If those exercise tapes from Leslie, Jackie, Jillian and the various other svelte lovelies were at all entertaining and didn't actually require coordination, the Couch Potato might not have joined the ranks of hikers. When you try exercising at home alone, there is no possibility that you can live up to the image you see on the video. Besides, how many of us actually have the room required to move about and do all of the gyrations shown on videos? The Couch Potato was always bumping into things and having to watch out for furniture. She was never going to show her face in a gymnastics class!

While hiking, you usually see people in all states of fitness. This is certainly less intimidating than the gorgeously coiffed, forever-youthful exercise gurus who never even seem to sweat. Plus, you don't need to memorize routines or count "reps." The Couch Potato could never keep track of the routines and felt entirely inept. What she could do was put one foot in front of another. That's hiking—or walking, if you prefer.

So, get up! That is the start. Since everything has to begin somewhere, getting up is about right as a first step. The hardest hike you'll ever take is out the door the first time.

Everything follows.

Plus, when you return home, the couch will still be there. It will seem even more comfy by comparison, a reward for your efforts!

What You Need to Hike

Technically, you don't need much equipment to hike.
But, being prepared is preferable. Now, you can do what
some people do, especially with children, which is to
get all dressed up and go out for a hike. Patent leather
shoes and party dresses are not recommended attire
for a hike. They hinder movement. Besides not being
practical, formal dress is not the easiest way to greet
nature. Showing off the latest name-brand fashion

accessories is also not essential. Nor is the birthday suit. That leads to sunburn and lots of bug bites. So, somewhere in the middle is a happy alternative.

So, what *should* you wear to the great outdoor encounter? Comfortable clothes that cover surfaces to protect from the elements are a good idea. Along those lines, sunscreen is also another good investment. A hat, sunglasses, hiking boots, and a few other items, which we'll discuss in the next chapter, are the first items you'll need.

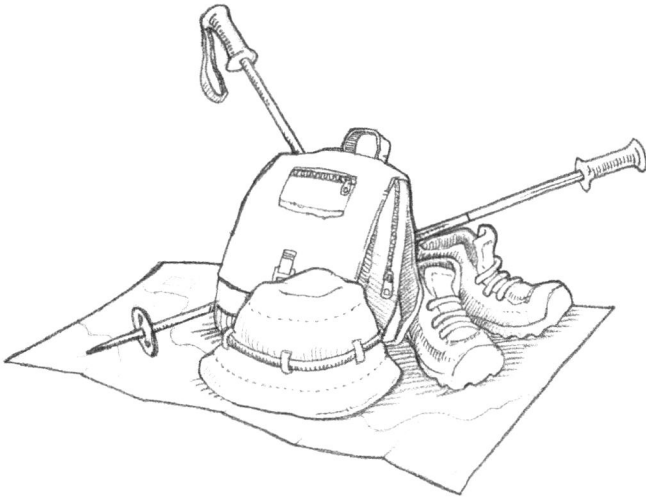

CHAPTER 2

Good Intentions:
Let's Shop!

AS A NEW HIKER, you will need to equip yourself for your days on the trail. You will be purchasing, or considering purchasing, hiking boots or shoes, hiking socks, poles, gloves, hat, and hydration equipment. (Flowers get watered—you need to be watered, too.)

When beginning a new project, especially one with possible traumatic outcomes, make lists to prepare for your shopping excursion and your hikes: What do I need? Where am I going? Who am I going with? When am I going?

Why am I doing this?!

After the lists are completed, you might freeze. This all looks very formidable. Given the chance to clean the house … talk with friends on the phone … pay bills … or almost *anything* else, a new hiker/ Couch Potato convert sometimes feels compelled to find alternate activities. This may be an okay thing to do at first.

To combat this avoidance behavior, a Couch Potato convert (in the future we will call this person a "hiker"—intentions are everything!) should do some preparatory activities that begin to change attitudes and lead to the inevitable first walk/hike. Most of us can walk. Putting one foot in front of the other is a habit we learned around one year of age. Consider hiking as the next step.

Hiking takes us further, makes us exert ourselves a bit, and gets us to expand our minds. It is meditation, challenge, and relaxation combined in one activity. Make the first hiking excursion a trip to a shoe store or outdoor products store to purchase hiking boots. After that, you'll need to consider acquiring socks, poles, gloves, and a hat.

What to Purchase: Your Mother *Does* Wear Combat Boots

Because feet take the brunt of the hiking effort, make your boot purchasing the first priority on your shopping list. Budgets and aesthetic preferences aside, it is most important that hiking boots/shoes fit comfortably. Unlike the ice skates that the Couch Potato's father laced so tightly that she could not feel her toes, hiking boots or shoes should give your feet room. That does not mean that they should be loose. Recently, the Couch Potato bought new hiking boots after several years of wearing some really comfortable ones. The old ones had worn out! This is a testimonial to the fact that she really had been hiking quite a bit.

Since the new ones were a bit too loose, every time she went down an incline, her feet slid forward and bumped her toes. That was painful after a while. So, having the boots fit just right is essential. (Try combating the sliding feet with thicker socks.)

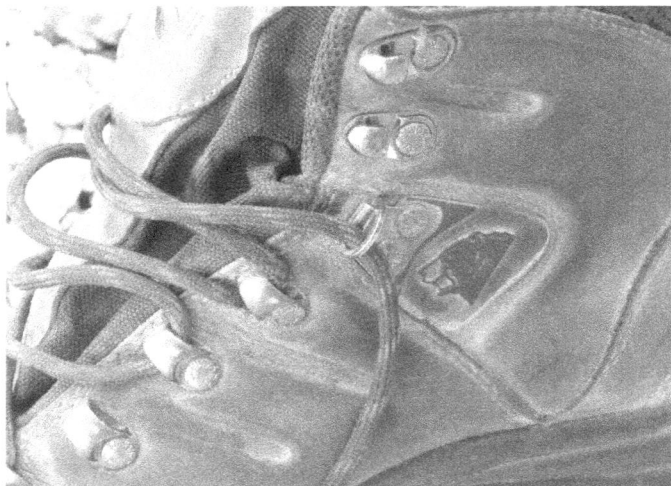

Don't hurry through your boot purchasing. Hiking boots have parts that require thorough examination. Make sure the tongue slips smoothly, with no bunching, into the space where you lace up the boot. Usually, hiking boots have a one-piece tongue that is fastened to the main body of the boot with a kind of pleated arrangement. This feature keeps out water, dust and anything that might fall in your shoe. See if you can lace the boot up with ease. Boots generally have a combination of metal eyelets (round), d-rings (metal openings shaped like the letter "D"), and speed hooks to fasten the boot. I find the d-rings and eyelets the easiest to work with, but most boots seem to have speed hooks, which are a metallic arrangement open on one edge, at the ankles. The lace can slip out of the speed hook if you don't anchor it firmly, so be sure you've fastened it well. After lacing the boots completely, walk in the boots while you are in the store.

You may feel like you're walking stiffly like a robot, but this is necessary to see if the boots really fit. Try walking up and down a step, if that is possible. Walk back and forth, turn sharply, and rotate around while standing in place. In other words, try maneuvering so you can see how you'll feel while on a trail. If the boots still feel good, that's a good sign. You'll be spending a lot of time in your boots, so you want to feel happy in them.

Another criteria is that the boots should come up the ankle a few inches for support. Having that extra height has saved the Couch Potato from turned ankles and additional sprains and strains a number of times. A high-backed boot may feel strange at first, but you will rapidly get used to it. Then, it feels great every time you go over an uneven path and the boot keeps your ankle safe and secure.

Every time she feels her ankle start to twist slightly, the high back keeps it straight. She usually ends the hike not even feeling the slight twist because her boot protected her ankle. Not getting hurt is a very good thing!

Leather is the best choice for the body of the boot because it protects feet from water and is sturdy enough to keep ankles from twisting easily. For the soles, the Couch Potato's husband swears by Vibram©, but she has had good luck with non-name-brand heavy rubber. This is a matter of preference and budget.

Recommending boot types is difficult since there are a number of great popular brands. There are two schools of thought. One is: Buy the best. That can cost several hundred dollars for a pair of boots. Which leads us to the other school of thought. Try hiking first before you help the national debt single-handedly. The Couch Potato's first boots were Dexter's. (*Disclaimer:* The author has not been paid to endorse this brand.) They felt really stiff at first. The Couch Potato's husband said that as long as they didn't hurt, they would eventually feel great. He was right! (See, we admit that a spouse can be right. This is a major occasion in some circles—to admit that a spouse can be right about something!)

The Couch Potato became very attached to her hiking boots. Every time she had an uneven surface to step over, tree limbs in the way, or muck to walk through, she loved them. Plain old walking shoes just paled in comparison after that. However, when she didn't bring a change of shoes for a post-hiking restaurant visit, she regretted it. The old childhood taunt, "Your mother wears combat boots!" *is* appropriate. Stomping around in hiking boots is *not attractive* in certain environments. Unless you are absolutely in need of attention, a shoe change is recommended after you have completed hiking for the day. One great thing about changing out of hiking boots is how light your feet feel after changing into almost any other footwear.

Did we mention that hiking boots are *heavy*? Well, they are.

But that is part of the mystique. Besides, it really isn't vanity. They do the work for which they are intended. (Remind us to tell you about how much fun a sprained ankle *isn't*.)

Remember, we are talking about "day hiking" vs. climbing Mt. Everest or hiking the entire Appalachian Trail from Maine to Georgia (roughly 2,174 miles).

The other alternative to "boots" is hiking "shoes." Although the Couch Potato has never worn them, a lot of people swear by hiking shoes, with dense rubber soles and grooves for gripping. For those of you who are looking for lighter (30 oz. weight vs. 60 oz.) footwear, the hiking shoe might well meet your needs. You're certainly going to reduce your "slip and slide" quotient as these are two steps up from sneakers (aka "tennis shoes") and have either sticky rubber soles, or lug rubber soles, i.e. Vibram® or Tru-Trak®, for example. For the uneven trails that you will definitely encounter, you are also better off with a stiffer shoe than a general athletic shoe for leisurely walks.

Another factor is the price. Although not necessarily a lot cheaper than some 6-inch high, full support hiking boots as the Couch Potato wears, the lack of material to produce them does factor into a lower retail cost.

Remember the earlier mention, "Stomping around in hiking boots is *not attractive* in certain environments?" With a hiking shoe, the *"attractiveness factor"* is not as much of a problem, as it looks more like a tennis shoe on steroids!

(Although some hikers prefer hiking shoes, the Couch Potato sticks by her endorsement of high backs.)

So, the choice is yours, just like getting off the couch for the first time and getting out there to *hike, hike, hike* … or at least, *hike, hike* … or maybe just, *hike!* Hiking is terrific that way: *everything is your choice.*

The one thing that will make absolutely no difference in whatever boot/shoe you select is the following:

There should be lots of padding in the shoes and on your feet!

Hiking Socks

You will also need to get hiking socks for additional cushioning. Hey, accessorization lets you use your talents to make hiking a harmonious experience. Heaven forbid you should wear your gray hiking socks with your beige pants.

Brands of hiking socks vary. The Couch Potato has had success with proprietary brands of hiking stores as well as name brands found in sporting goods stores. She hesitates to endorse any particular brand, but is open to convincing. The hiking socks you choose should have extra padding in the heel and toe areas. No matter what, the Couch Potato believes in being prepared. When the packaging says, "Light Hiking," ignore those and go up to the regular hiking level. So, indeed, be prepared. The Couch Potato was a Girl Scout.

Not a Pole-ish Joke

You really should invest in a hiking pole or two. Besides the fact that you will look sharp, you will actually find a pole helpful. When there is a slight incline or a rough patch to traverse, having poles keeps hikers steady. The type of pole the Couch Potato uses can also be a ski pole. It is adjustable for a person of almost any height. When finished hiking, it telescopes down to a short, storable length. The version the Couch Potato uses has a strap that you put your wrist through, as well as a rubbery grip.

Before investing in the pole, the Couch Potato tried using sturdy sticks of various lengths. Although serviceable, using sticks meant she had to keep one hand devoted to holding onto the stick. With the strap on the current model, she can use both hands quickly if she needs to grab on to a hold or move something out of her way. When out on trails, she has seen people who don't use a pole struggling, especially if they are holding a water bottle. So, keeping one hand free is helpful.

We highly recommend using a hiking pole. One pole is all the Couch Potato uses, as she shares the two-pole set with her husband.

Hand in Glove

If your hands tend to perspire, using a glove (or two if you decide to use two poles) is recommended. Gloves are leather or a mesh-leather combination that can be breathable. The Couch Potato actually uses a fingerless, weightlifting glove that she picked up at a local discount retailer. It keeps her hand on the pole securely.

So, boots, socks, poles, gloves. Do we have everything yet? Not quite!

The Potato in the Hat

Wear a hat. Wear a hat that covers your ears and shades your face and your neck. Although a lot of the accoutrements for hiking are open to many choices, we believe that keeping your skin protected is very important. The Couch Potato favors the floppy-brimmed type that has a layer to protect you from the sun. There are several brands of this type of hat, but they all usually have a chin strap to help them stay on. On a windy day, you'll really appreciate that. The Couch Potato's hat stays on while other hikers' ball caps go sailing by in the breeze.

Also, a ball cap is not a good choice because it doesn't cover your ears or neck. And, your ears and neck are not immune from sun damage. Other hats might be more comfortable or lighter, but a floppy-brimmed hat of the type we're advocating really keeps the sun out of your face. The hats don't make a fashion statement. They come in beige or khaki, generally. By the time you get to choosing a hat, you'll probably just want to get hiking, anyway.

Okay, so you think you'll look like a dork. Fuhgeddaboudit! Go for the sun blocked look. It's much more attractive than bright red, peeling skin—which brings us to—

Protection from the Elements

Three more things: (We know, this seems like a lot to haul, but that's what all of the pockets are for!)

Sun

Use *sunscreen* on your exposed skin—arms, hands, wrists, legs, etc. Just because you're not at the beach doesn't mean you can't get sunburned. Why add to your miseries? Find the greaseless kind of sunscreen that is at least SPF 15 (we highly recommend using SPF 30) and rub it on before you set out on your trail. Hey, you don't really want to be a *baked* potato! (We know, very corny. But we couldn't resist!)

Recently, Couch Potato's husband forgot to put sun block on his head during a hike. His hat kept blowing off. Three weeks later, his head finally stopped peeling.

Bugs

When within a mile of bugs, the Couch Potato tends to be the one person who will get bitten. So, she also recommends that you use a rub on (it can be controlled better) or spray version of *bug repellent*. Huge welts are not appealing as body décor. You will be glad if you wear these protections.

First Aid

As a Girl Scout, the Couch Potato also endorses bringing a small *first aid kit.* This could be put in various pockets or a backpack. Plan to bring disinfectant (the sealed packets of wipes work well), bandages, antibiotic ointment and a small pair of scissors.

Now, this begins to sound intimidating. Why go outside and put yourself in a possible situation where you can get sunburned, bug-bitten, or even injured? Good question!

Well, we guess because the good outweighs the possible bad—especially if you take the precautions

that we've suggested. It certainly makes you a better-prepared hiker. And, unless you are forced to live in a bubble environment, you most likely will be required to go outside. The Couch Potato gets bug-bitten just going to her car in a parking lot. The bugs just love her!

As to what clothes to wear, loose fitting clothes are great. Lots of pockets are helpful to store the odds and ends you probably will want. The odds and ends can include a compass, a trail map, protein bar, trail mix, the first aid kit previously mentioned and many other items. Pockets with fastening material (ok, Velcro®) are particularly helpful so nothing gets lost.

Are we ready? Not quite. In addition to a water supply, you will also need to decide where to hike. This all seems like a lot to deal with. But, it's worth it! And, most of this is only a one-time effort. After you've made these choices, you don't need to decide any of this again.

CHAPTER 3

Water, Water – Everywhere?

YOU MAY BE HIKING AROUND a large body of water, but drinking from it is not recommended. Since we're only talking about day hiking here, we don't recommend that you haul water-purification systems along. So, bring water from home. If you drink bottled water, bring that. For many years, the Couch Potato brought a water bottle with a strap that she slung over her shoulder. If you like cold water, using a wide-mouthed bottle will allow you to use ice. Some bottles even allow you to insert frozen cold packs to keep the bottle cool.

Recently, she treated herself to a "hydrator." This is a fancy name for a water bladder that is part of a backpack-like or waistpack-like set up that leaves your hands free. A tube comes from the bladder that allows you to sip as you walk. This set up is great, since having hands free is a major good thing when hiking. The brand the Couch Potato purchased is a Camelbak (she has not been paid to endorse this product). Her husband chose a Deuter brand system. (He hasn't been paid to endorse this, either.) We just tried on the backpacks until we found one that felt comfortable. Comfort is everything.

Our one complaint, since we live in a very warm climate, is that the water that stays in the tube between sips tends to get warm as it is exposed. New models deal with that issue by insulating the tube that extends to your mouth. Since it is not a world-shaking problem, we will probably engineer a "fix" for our older model's design.

Having no water on a hike *is* a world-shaking problem. We know, because on one hike, the Couch Potato forgot to bring water. She and her husband started out, got down the path a bit, and then realized their mistake. They should have gone back for the water. They didn't. Instead, the Couch Potato was very thirsty and parched. A parched Potato is not a pretty sight! She never did that again.

If it seems like the Potato has made mistakes, well, she certainly has. However, you don't need to make the same mistakes she made. You can learn from her experience. Make your own mistakes!

So, now we've gotten our water bottles ready. Quantity of water? Well, this depends on how far and long you're preparing to hike. The Couch Potato usually takes a two-quart or two-liter pack, which suffices for the one to three hours she usually hikes. For longer hikes, which most novice hikers won't be attempting right away, consider bringing up to a gallon of water per day per person. Medical recommendations are for two to three liters per day (which may not adjust for activity). Also, medical sources seem to agree that thirst is not a good indicator of when you need water. Don't wait to feel thirsty before you drink. Adjust accordingly for climate, your size, and how active you are. In Arizona, where the Couch Potato lives, even leaving the house without water for a simple errand can be a bad idea. So, bring water. Bring extra. Never leave home without it.

The Couch Potato also brings some food—trail mix, nuts, protein bars or other portable food. We try for snacks that are easy and essential, so we're prepared. (See Chapter 8, "Recipes for the Couch Potato" later in the book.)

And, about water—if it looks like it might rain, do not start a long hike. In her ten-plus years of hiking, only once has the Couch Potato been caught on the trail in a downpour. That was a scary experience, as there was lightning. Lightning *is* a force to be reckoned with. Get out of the rain. This is a good day to watch the soap operas you recorded.

So, are we finally prepared to hike? NO!

We need to decide where and when to hike.

BEFORE YOU HIKE

DISCLAIMER—If you are as sedentary as the Couch Potato was, it would be a good idea to visit your doctor before you begin your hiking experience. The author is not responsible for the reader's health and cannot be held responsible for any accidents or mishaps that occur. Please take precautions and do not overdo.

We're a litigious society—you can't blame us for putting in the legal stuff.

CHAPTER 4

Things to Learn from Hiking

DECIDING WHERE TO HIKE is a very personal thing. Books abound on the subject. Often, the books give you a rating on the difficulty of the hike. Don't believe them! When a book says that a hike is "easy," a Couch Potato will most likely find the hike harder than "easy." Likewise for "moderate" and "difficult." We do not want to have our friends and fellow hikers have to practice their CPR moves on us. So, for a first hike, try a neighborhood park.

Research where you might like to hike, even the neighborhood park. Research is easy using the Internet or asking others what their experience has been. A trip to a local sporting goods company or community center might also yield some places to hike and other people who like to hike and can give you insights on the "good, the bad and the ugly" of local hikes.

If you've done your research, you'll know how far the hike will be and what you might encounter. For instance, the trail might be a multi-use trail that also allows bicyclists and even horses. If that is the case, plan to move aside when other users come along.

A half-mile is about enough for a first try. We highly recommend taking the gear we've mentioned. Although gearing up for a half-mile may seem like a lot of work, it is always helpful to know that you are prepared. Once you've tried the half-mile, then you have an idea about pacing and your stamina.

Our rule of thumb is to decide how long you want to hike, then hike out for about half that amount of time. This means that you have allowed enough time for your return. If the trail is circular (or a "loop") you would make note of the distance and decide if you can do the whole route. Otherwise, just go half as far as planned to hike and return using the same route. This is not rocket science, but it is good to go prepared and with a plan.

Having a trail map can be extremely helpful. Usually at the beginning of a trail—the "trailhead"— there is a trail map posted. National Parks have maps available and sometimes states, counties and cities provide printed maps. If there is a map posted, but none available to take with you, examine the map carefully. If there is more than one trail, they will usually be shown in different colors on the map. Great concept—color coding! You will then often find that trees or other signs are "blazed" or painted in the color of its particular trail. Sometimes, there are even trail signs with arrows. And, trails might be indicated by "cairns," or heaps of stones, which have been purpose- fully placed to show the trail.

So, when you see trail maps, that will give you an indication of the hike's length and difficulty. Or not!

An example. At a state park, we saw signs for the "Circumferential Trail." The sign said "2 miles." With the experience we had, that seemed possible. What the sign didn't say was that the trail connected to three other trails that would make the miles to hike a total of five miles. We weren't really prepared. And, oh, those five miles seemed long. But, the hike was around a very pretty lake, so we paced ourselves and wound up enjoying it.

Couch Potato has mentioned "WE." This is not the "royal" we. Definitely, always, without exception, bring a hiking buddy. **Do Not Hike Alone**. If anything were to happen, you would want someone to call for help. Bringing a cell phone is a good idea as well, but cannot replace another person. Cell phones may not have reception in all areas. (See how those items in all of those pockets are multiplying?)

This is not to imply that something *will* happen. It is just better to be prepared. And, it is certainly a good way to get to know people better. Check out that person you've been dating, significant other or good friend. You'll find out a lot about them from hiking with them.

Do they snap branches aside without regard to where they'll land (e.g. in your face)? Do they drink up their water and want yours, too? Do they whine

and complain about everything? Life is a test. And hiking with someone is a great test.

There is etiquette on the trail. You should move aside if people are coming from the opposite direction. If you let them pass, it makes it easier for everyone. If your hiking buddy consistently doesn't yield to others, he or she is a pushy type. It is better to know this while hiking before you are "hitched" for life.

So, hiking is a way to learn about people. One of the things hiking lets you enjoy is nature. If your hiking buddy never wants to stop and smell the roses, look at the ripples on the lake, listen for the sounds of the woods, or pause to identify the native flora and fauna, that may be the way he or she is in the rest of his/her life. Do you want to spend your time with someone with no poetry in his or her soul—or appreciation of the world?

That is a question to be answered in another book on another day. For the Couch Potato, hiking has taught her about others' patience, stamina, understanding, and resourcefulness. Amazing! All that from one jaunt in the woods!

You also learn a lot about yourself. When she has taken on a long trail with bravado and has been unprepared, the Couch Potato has come to regret it. Once, blithely, she said, "Come on, let's take this longer trail." It was a warm day and other people were turning back. When she found herself faint, she realized that it had been a long time since she had eaten and she needed food. Since she had brought a protein bar along, she stopped to eat and felt much better. Though the hike had felt torturous, she felt a sense of exultation and elation when she was done. Also, she took one of the finest photos she had ever taken that day.

Also, check out the restrooms before you head out on a trail. Unless you are hiking in primitive locations, there will usually be a restroom in the vicinity. A small container of waterless hand cleaner is helpful, as some facilities are the flushless type, so there is no water available. Bringing some toilet tissue along is a wise precaution as well. (Again, those multiple pockets can come in handy!)

We absolutely recommend using the restroom before starting your hike. 'Nuff said on that topic. We could probably write another book on trail restroom accommodations.

And, here we are! We've lived through all of this and survived to tell about it. We've enjoyed some wonderful hikes that we will describe to you. As we haven't been to all 50 of the United States, we can't tell you about every hike in every place. She does know that as a former Couch Potato, she does not attempt difficult hikes. So, she can endorse the hikes that you may want to try.

And, why are we doing this? Well, there may be a certain amount of masochism in this pursuit, as in many leisure activities. An example: The Couch Potato's relative was (jokingly) told that he alone would qualify for the *group* rate for the doctor's services since he'd been seen so many times. Too many softball injuries!

To hit you with a cliché: nothing ventured, nothing gained. And wouldn't you rather gain experience from hiking? (Not weight from staying put and nibbling while lounging on the couch?) So, it is time to shake up your routine and get up off the couch!

As the Couch Potato has previously indicated, her injuries have not been related to hiking. Risk a little. Hiking is worth it! Besides, we look so cool in our hiking attire!

Getting to the Hikes

Couch Potato's first real hike was probably more like a walk. But then, that is progress. If you move from the horizontal and walk, applaud yourself.

She truly doesn't recall when she first started hiking. When she first purchased hiking boots, she *felt* like she was truly hiking. If you walk on a paved path that goes on for a distance, that qualifies as hiking. But to the Couch Potato, a dirt path just feels more "real."

When you hike on a dirt path with tree roots to step over, you feel as if you are now an explorer. You share something with the trailblazers of yore. You're discovering the world. It feels fresh and new, a place to pit your energies and stamina against Mother Nature. It is even more thrilling than handling the remote and flipping to a channel where you discover a favorite movie. So, you now have a feeling of why you might actually wish to get out there.

The feeling of hiking shares something with the competitive spirit of mankind. (No, we are not intending to be politically incorrect. We mean *"man*kind" in the cosmic sense.) You have challenges. You have strengths. You want to succeed. If a trail map says it takes forty-five minutes to accomplish a particular hike, you want to finish in forty minutes. But, you still want to feel the joy of succeeding on your own terms. If something catches your attention and you want to observe it, you won't care if it takes you fifty-seven minutes to reach your destination.

Also, you learn something about your own stamina. When the Couch Potato feels that her energy needs a boost, she uses another strategy that she devised. She counts her steps until she reaches ten. When reaching ten, she pauses and takes a few deep breaths and looks around. Taking note of any interesting plants or animals, staying very still, she observes without disturbing nature's true inhabitants. Then, she makes another mental contract to take another ten steps. In this way, she breaks up what seems like a long stretch into more manageable chunks. Look around so that you can actually see nature!

If you find a slightly hilly area, allow yourself to rest at intervals. We are not superheroes and do not

need to prove anything to anyone. Most of all, if you do not feel well when you are hiking, let your hiking partner know. (Remember, ALWAYS HIKE WITH SOMEONE. This could involve joining a hiking club. You never know—someone you meet in the hiking club could wind up being your hiking and life partner!)

Stop and rest when you feel the need. If you need to, end your hike. RESTING IS ALLOWED!

Learning from Hikes

One of the Couch Potato's favorite hikes is at a park near Richmond, Virginia. The hike is in *Rockwood Park*, a county park that has a number of paths that originate from different locations. There is a main, paved path, but there are numerous dirt paths to try. You can change the direction you walk and come upon a lake from two different directions. There is only one steep path that has a section that goes up at about a 40-degree angle, but after the steep part, the trail turns. The reward for your efforts in climbing this steeper section of trail is to reach a shady spot around the bend at the top. At the spot is an informational plaque that tells how this particular location had been used by early settlers to keep ice frozen—even in summer. Discoveries like this keep life interesting. The Couch Potato generally takes a slope like that in one concerted effort, then allows herself a luxurious rest at the top while she reads the plaque.

You can tell when you are in better condition by how winded you are by a slope you've hiked up before. If you are huffing and puffing, you will know you need to get in shape. By the end of the hiking season, you won't be panting and feeling foolish if other hikers are in the vicinity.

We are not climbing Mt. Everest here! Our goal is to get out there, see some birds, Nature (yes, with a capital "N") and get away from the things that raise our blood pressure back in our cocoons. While hiking, as the Couch Potato has, you might see deer, squirrels, birds of various types, incredible rock formations, and inspiring mountains vistas. Many views have made her pause—not because she was out of breath, but because she found something that took her breath away with its beauty. The most amazing thing is to see a hummingbird—a tiny whir of motion that hovers by the flowers and moves on, almost the way you'd expect Tinker Bell from *Peter Pan* to move.

A stream with water rippling over the rocks is another scene she would never see perched on her couch. Or an old barn that no longer houses animals or stores grains. Or a lovely wildflower. Sometimes, just the way a tree's shadow looks can be the reason to pause and observe. It is all so inspiring that she wishes she could draw. Instead, since she is not much of a sketcher, she brings a camera and takes photos. Then, she can capture the beauty of her hike on film

or digitally. If you go hiking and bring a camera and take photos, it also will serve as proof that you really did go hiking!

Once, the Couch Potato thought she was going to be hiking with a group. It turned out to be rock-climbing with a group, a totally different effort. (Climbing implies going *up*!) She met some great guys, but this is now one of those stories she tells when she wants to recount what she did in her wild, crazy, younger years! The rock-climbing convinced her that it was not her outdoor activity of choice. The guys may have been great, but being on a ledge a hundred-plus feet up was not her preferred way to spend time. She got down safely, but she didn't like to have that far to fall!

Hiking and walking seem so much safer!

Yodeling in the Woods

Yodel? Well, why not? If you are in need of a stress reliever, yodel, sing at the top of your lungs, chant, whistle or make any number of noises that you might not be likely to do back in public. In their usual urban or suburban settings, people can be inhibited in the sounds they make. Out in the middle of a hike, you might offend the wildlife, but they aren't going to object. At times, the Couch Potato indulges in a chorus or two of "The Happy Wanderer"—"valderee! valderah!"—etc. when out hiking. Her husband ignores her or pretends he is not with her until she stops singing. She persists. The freedom to express yourself is another benefit of hiking. The one form of expression to avoid, unless absolutely necessary, is screaming. On the off chance that someone is in the vicinity, a scream could send the wrong message.

Alternatives in Life:
Walking for the Couch Potato

And, if this all seems like too much, there's a fall back position! You can go walking. You can choose urban areas and walk around the block. You can walk around an indoor shopping mall in bad weather. You can go up and down the stairs in your house or apartment. You can walk out to the mailbox and back several times. In other words, move!

If you are the competitive type, even if it is competing against yourself, you can purchase a pedometer and record how far you've walked. Next time, walk farther!

A good thing about walking or hiking is that you can join groups to share that pastime. Maybe you'll even meet your life partner in a hiking group! Choose your group wisely. Scope out what the group's goals are, their level of expertise and whether they welcome newcomers.

The whole idea is to get out there, get some exercise, and improve your cardiovascular functioning. We could fill these pages with frightening statistics

about health concerns. People could counterattack with stories about how major runner "gurus" drop dead while running. None of this is productive. What is productive is to choose a way to get some exercise. If it doesn't feel like exercise, has additional benefits like photographic opportunities, or doesn't require you to memorize complicated routines, be happy.

Find your recreational opportunity and enjoy it!

CHAPTER 5

Hiking with Two- and Four-Legged Companions

THERE ARE TIMES WHEN you might consider hiking, but your child or pet is around and you don't want to leave them behind. This can work! Actually, you might get even more exercise, because you should be prepared to carry your infant, small child or dog. So, no excuses! You can hike with a child or animal, but you will need to make a few more preparations. And, no matter how tempting it might be, please

NEVER leave your child or dog in the car alone with or without the windows rolled up. They should accompany you, even to the restroom.

With another adult along, you can certainly have them stay with the child or dog, but even though it may be tempting, NEVER LEAVE YOUR CHILD OR DOG ALONE IN THE CAR. Yes, we repeat ourselves. We have seen children and dogs left in closed cars and feel the need to repeat. We would like to think that readers of this book will all be wise and practical people who would never consider endangering their loved ones, be they children or pets. We have found that on even slightly warm days, cars get hot. We once saw it take a long time for a Park Ranger to get to a vehicle where a dog was locked inside. We did not enjoy our hike that day until we saw that the dog was safe.

Taking an Infant or Small Child Hiking

An infant can be carried in a backpack arrangement, of which there are many excellent brands and models. (See Appendix II.) As you prepare for hiking by wearing a hat and smearing on sun block, also prepare the baby. Make regular stops and offer the baby water. Be especially careful when you attempt trails with uneven surfaces, since you want your footing to be sure and steady.

Don't overdo it! Sometimes, babies will sleep through anything, but you want to make sure they are safe. If you have a long hike planned, you might consider leaving the baby home with a babysitter.

Small children who can't walk far on their own should be given the option of a carrier, as well. If they are past the toddler stage and can walk steadily, offer the child a chance to walk. Make regular stops, using the time to point out birds, flowers, and other noteworthy natural elements. This will encourage your child to like hiking, too. They will consider it an important part of their own life, establishing a great pattern for them. See, hiking is a healthy pursuit for you and makes you a great influence!

Hiking with Dogs

Dogs can join you for a hike. If you are new to the experience, so are they. However, they can enjoy the outdoors with very little adaptation. Bring water along for them. To offer the water, try a collapsible water dish, a small cup, or a bottle you can squeeze.

Be prepared for small dogs to let you know when they've had enough walking. Then, you'll need to carry them. Larger dogs will probably leave you in the dust, if you let them. They will be delighted to explore.

We do recommend that you keep your dog on a leash. Recently on a multi-use trail, we saw a dachshund almost get run over by a bicyclist. Dachshunds don't move that quickly.

CHAPTER 6

Hikes We've Liked

ORGANIZED FROM EAST TO WEST, we have included hikes we know personally. All of the detailed hikes we include (except those labeled otherwise) are ones we consider easy and manageable for new hikers. (Couch Potato "easy," not the "easy" labeled in books for experienced hikers.)

Although we will try to recommend hikes that have no fee, there is a fee for national parks. If you know that you will be traveling a great deal in one year, or have a national park near you that you could frequent, buying the National Park's annual pass is a great option. Then, you'll have unlimited admission for you and your traveling companion or family to the National Parks for one year. See Appendix I for more specifics about each hike and how to find other hiking locations.

Hikes in the East

FREEDOM TRAIL (BOSTON)–Massachusetts

The Freedom Trail is a great urban hike. The hard part is finding a place to park your car (said in Boston-ese as "Pahk yahr cahr"). Otherwise, get to Boston via the MTA (Metropolitan Transport Authority) trains, which run regularly. Following the Freedom Trail, the red-brick line, which travels through downtown Boston to Charleston, you will have the opportunity to see many sites of historical interest and do some walking. The Bunker Hill Monument, which is free, is run by the National Parks department and provides a fabulous view of Boston Harbor. This "jaunt" up the 294 steps to the top can be your final challenge during your walk. When you get to the top, you feel triumphant—and probably winded! Who said hiking can't be done in urban settings?!

Also on the Freedom Trail you can see Paul Revere's Home (fee for the tour); enjoy shops, outside activities, and restaurants at Faneuil Hall; view Old

North Church where Paul Revere's midnight ride began (bring your history books!); tour the USS Constitution (known as "Old Ironsides"), which is the oldest commissioned warship afloat in the world; and experience other sights and sounds of Boston. Allow the day, since there is so much to see, or just pick a few sights. Either way, you'll get a good view of Boston and a great hike!

C&O (Chesapeake and Ohio) CANAL–Washington, D.C. and Maryland

Following the banks of the Potomac, the 184.5 miles of the C&O Canal, is a National Parks Service Historical Park. We are not suggesting that you consider hiking the entire length. If you live in the vicinity, choose a segment, which can be as short as you would like. The towpath, which hugs the Potomac, is flat and level and provides great scenery. In addition to the seasonal flora and fauna, old aqueducts, canal locks, Great Falls, and historical buildings and markers show you the way of life that ended when barges stopped being the main method of transportation and commerce. The towpaths are multi-use trails, so be aware of cyclists.

WALLER MILL PARK–Virginia

Just outside of Williamsburg, Virginia, is the lovely city park, Waller Mill Park. There is a lot to enjoy there even if you don't want to hike. Reasonable canoe rentals give you the opportunity to use your upper body. You'll then get a look at a lovely reservoir that stretches in many directions with many inlets.

But, since we're focusing on hiking, let's talk about hiking at Waller Mill. It's wonderful! There are trails that follow the water and are shaded by trees, and others that wander past picnic areas. You can also make your hike in a more traveled area that goes near a highway. There are rarely many people hiking around, so you can enjoy the peace, quiet, and flora and fauna. It is quite inspirational. None of the trails are particularly difficult, so take your time and decide how far you want to go. If this hike sounds appealing, further details and directions are contained in Appendix I in the back of the book.

ROCKWOOD PARK–Virginia

Nestled in a residential area in Chesterfield County, Virginia, Rockwood Park is one of those suburban parks that just feels like a good place to be. Families enjoy the park because it has picnic areas, ball fields, archery targets, and other amenities. We like it because it has accessible trails that are near parking lots. The trails are shaded, an attribute that is pleasant in the warmer months, and offer a lot of variety. You can see water, creatures (nothing of the slithery, scary variety), birds, and you will still be only twenty minutes away from civilization at the most. Several trails meander throughout the park, one of which has blacktop. The trees have a "blaze"—a colored slash painted on—that, for the most part, makes a trail easy to follow.

Being able to hike for twenty minutes, or as long as an hour when we just wanted to get outdoors, made this a great choice when we lived in the Richmond, Virginia area. More specifics about Rockwood Park can be found in Appendix I.

A Central Hike

COMO PARK, St. Paul–Minnesota

Another urban hike, Como Park is a beautiful setting with an arboretum, zoo, lake and carousel. While hiking shoes or walking shoes would suffice here, the extensive hiking gear we usually recommend is probably not needed. However, we just had to include this idyllic park. To get the maximum healthful effect, walk quickly around the park, taking in the attractions. Then, stroll back through the individual settings that are of interest to you. There are enough slopes to give you a bit of exercise, while offering a lovely feast for your eyes. Children will especially love this park, since the carousel, zoo, and amenities are kid-friendly. During the summer months, a Japanese garden can be seen in the arboretum. The arboretum and zoo request a small donation.

Hikes in the West

SOUTH MOUNTAIN PARK–Phoenix, Arizona

The largest city park in the United States, South Mountain Park, is just off the main interstate (I10) not far from Phoenix Sky Harbor Airport in Arizona. A desert park, the hikes have desert scenery, views of the city of Phoenix, and many desert residents to share your hike. Recently, we saw roadrunners hustling back and forth across our trail. Too fast to capture them moving on film, the roadrunners were not quite like the cartoon character that torments Wile E. Coyote.

Some of the trails are challenging (not so easy), but a few are on flat, level ground and have great desert scenery. Just outside of suburban Phoenix, it is amazing to see the desert vistas with saguaro cactus, prickly pear, and other desert landscaping five minutes from shopping centers.

Note: The City of Phoenix recently implemented a parking fee for day hiking on the Pima Canyon trailhead at South Mountain Park, with a parking pass to download and display in vehicles. Learn more about this park in Appendix I.

ZION NATIONAL PARK–Utah

Utah has some of the most breathtaking parks in the country. Zion National Park, in Springdale, Utah, is one of the most inspiring. Magnificent rock formations

have trails near their bases that allow you to walk about near streams, waterfalls, and wildlife.

Some of the trails are more challenging than others, but try easy hikes first and see if you can manage more difficult paths later. You can watch rock climbers as they tether themselves to the rock faces and work their way slowly to the top. Flowers bloom under overhangs in areas where it would seem impossible for things to grow.

There is a fee for this National Park. It is certainly worth it! Learn more about Zion National Park in Appendix I.

MUIR WOODS—California

One of the most meditative places to walk/hike that we have ever been, Muir Woods is a small, but wonderful, place populated by old-growth redwoods, just north of San Francisco, California. The park is easy to navigate with flat trails, some of which are even accessible to those in wheelchairs. Muir Woods is beautiful in a way few places can be. You can just feel the age and wisdom of the trees, with light filtering through the branches.

There are only a total of six miles of trails, but they are in one-half hour to one-and-a-half hour loops that let you meditate on life and the harmony of nature. To be surrounded by the oldest living things on the planet, this is the place to be. The old hiker's chestnut, "Take only photographs, leave only footprints" has been amended to "Take only memories and photographs…" This is very fitting. You almost feel as if you should whisper while you are there. Picnicking, biking and dogs are not allowed in the park.

Being a national monument, there is a small admission fee. (Buy a National Parks pass if you'll be traveling a lot in one year. Muir Woods is free if you have a National Park's pass.)

How to Find Hiking Opportunities

We recognize that the above hikes are not an exhaustive list, but we chose them as representative of the type of hikes that would be good experiences for new hikers. See Appendix I for more on the hikes listed above.

To find more hikes suitable for your area, look online for "Hikes" or "Parks," adding your city or area in the search term. Your local library or outdoor supply stores are also excellent resources. See Appendix II for the outdoor supply stores.

As the Couch Potato community develops online, we will feature recommended hikes from other Couch Potatoes who have succeeded in getting up off the couch! See *http://hiking.forthecouchpotato.com* to suggest hikes you have enjoyed and to offer details or find a suggestion for your area. We will be forming Couch Potato Hiking groups in many communities, so take a look at the Web site!

CHAPTER 7

Strains, Sprains and Pains

THE OBJECT OF HIKING is to be healthier and to enjoy nature. Despite the best of intentions and preparation, however, sometimes a hiker can become injured. While we are not medical professionals, this hiker has had some first aid training.

(*Disclaimer:* We are not attempting to give medical advice, but suggestions. For entertainment value only. Does that meet the legal level of disclaimer? We certainly hope so!)

The strains and pains of hiking may not always involve a physical injury, either. First, let's talk honestly about strains and pains on the trail.

Hiking Strains and Pains

Imagine spending your time with someone who is not "in tune" with you. If you join a hiking group, that could become a reality. Make sure you do know what you are getting into.

If your experience is limited, it can be a good thing to be part of a group. Others in a group will have knowledge to share. But, and this is a BIG but, you may wind up with people who are show-offs, know-it-alls, pranksters and not beginners like you. Have the assertiveness to speak up if you find the others in your group are attempting a pace or a hike that you cannot handle.

In the Couch Potato's wild youth, she joined a hike with several people from an established hiking group. Without proper shoes or equipment, she was ill-prepared for what turned out to be a climbing group. Ever eager to socialize, she was determined to persevere. And, it was *definitely* severe.

At one point when the four-member group discovered that the path they had chosen was intersecting with a very large hornets' nest, the group leader decided to find another route. That seemed like a prudent idea, but it required that the very green hiker/climber undo the ropes that were tying her to the more experienced climbers and stand on a very narrow ledge for more than an hour. She could hear everyone calling, so she knew she was not alone. She started chanting to herself, "We will be fine." But, the slope was steep and the afternoon light was dwindling.

This was all taking much longer than she had anticipated. Having been thirsty, she drank quite a bit of water. Help!—no restroom on the narrow ledge. Try not to think of it? Yes, just about as effective as trying not to think about the pink elephant in the room. Can't stop thinking about that old pink elephant, right? So, eventually, the group leader found the way, a rope was lowered to the somewhat numb hiker, and they all wound up at the top of the cliff. Safe!

To go back down the slope in the near darkness would have been foolhardy. When she learned about the path that was an easy hike back to the base, she realized that she was not destined to become a climber. Somehow, if she had known about the path to start with—she would have met the group at the top with refreshments. No perching on the narrow ledge would have been required.

This is all a true story and a roundabout way of saying: find out what the others you hike with have in mind. Ask the group what possible difficulties the hike will entail. How far do they intend to go? Are the other hikers experts? Do they know you are a newbie? Know what to expect before you venture out with the group. As they say, you'll thank us for this!

Reminder: Apart from what the group is planning, you should: bring water, trail mix, etc. and take care of any bathroom needs.

Real Pains

Since you have anticipated all of your needs—(right?)—you should not have any major surprises, other than amazing views of nature. Your hiking shoes or boots should offer you the protection you need to prevent any foot or leg injuries. Your hiking pole should give you the extra oomph you need to make it up rises and over rough spots. You are prepared!

Well, sometimes, you encounter some trail conditions you cannot anticipate. On a hike in the absolutely amazing Bryce Canyon National Park in Utah, this hiker did not realize that it would be wet and slippery. The tall, towering cliffs of the park made the paths icy and dangerous. The path looked clear, but was deceptively slick. Suddenly, her feet slipped out from under her and she went flying! Landing with a thud, the part injured the most was her dignity. The camera got a little muddy and scraped up, too. Throughout that day, the mud on her bottom was a badge of honor.

Now, back in her room that evening, she did not have the absolutely essential item that she uses to combat aches and pains: frozen green peas!

Ode to Frozen Green Peas

If you have an ache or pain, the best technique to make you feel better is a bag of frozen green peas!

(Again—disclaimer—this is not meant as medical advice. If you are injured and have severe pain, please seek a doctor … who recommends frozen green peas.)

After a number of non-hiking related injuries over the years, the Couch Potato has found frozen green peas to be a boon to restoring pain-free functioning. After trying icepacks, other frozen vegetables and items, frozen green peas are still the best. They contour to the part that is sore and, just when they are starting to defrost a bit, they can go back in the freezer. The Couch Potato keeps two-pound bags on hand at home. Since we do not ever eat those particular bags of peas, they can stay around indefinitely, being refrozen numerous times. The larger bags provide more coverage, but for smaller parts, a one-pound bag could work fine, too.

Plan to place the frozen peas on the sore spot for about ten minutes on each hour/fifty minutes off. By the third hour, you'll probably have the swelling down and the pain will be lessened as a result.

Even frozen corn just does not equal the properties of frozen green peas since their edges wind up feeling uncomfortable. They just do not contour as well.

Pain in Hiking?

Although the Couch Potato has now hiked for years, the only sprain she ever had was from non-hiking related activities. Inelegantly, she twisted and sprained her foot while stepping in a pothole. She also misjudged a step on a dark stairwell and again sprained the same ankle.

So, no, hiking has not been injurious to this former Couch Potato's health!

Now, pain can be another thing. Landing on the slippery path in Bryce Canyon or losing footing on another trail, she has experienced some pain. (Taking along one of those instant icepacks can be good to use for such an occasion, by the way.)

For most of her hiking, she has arrived intact with no bruises, scrapes or other unintended souvenirs.

Crossing a flowing stream has probably been the most hazardous effort she has attempted, and she was able to manage quite well, jumping from rock to rock.

Advice from the Trail

Pace yourself. If you approach life like an overachiever, it's time to relax and enjoy a slower pace.

If you're having a bad day and start out not feeling optimal, consider whether you should be hiking that day. But sometimes a little trip into nature can be just the thing to make you forget what was bothering you, a real antidote for the world's pressures.

Be prepared. Yes, indeed the scout motto. Bring the water, proper shoes, the trail food, the hat and the other essentials. If you don't, you may well regret it.

About cell phones: good to have, but save them for use if an emergency crops up. Half the time, the hiking paths just don't seem to have great reception anyway. You need to disconnect from the world to enjoy your hike. If you're waiting to hear about an emergency situation, maybe you should be helping elsewhere.

If this all sounds like your mother hitting you with good common sense … well take it as that. Common sense is misnamed and does not appear to be that common. The little girl in a party dress and patent shoes on the hiking trail—and we really have seen that!—tells us that people do not always do the sensible thing.

Last piece of advice: Take a hike! We don't mean that rudely, as when people tell you to get lost. We do suggest that hiking is one of the few accessible hobbies that you can have where you don't need to compete with iconic sports figures.

You don't need to buy expensive equipment. You don't need to commit a whole day to "accomplishing" something. You don't need to *finish* a trail. Seriously. This is an empowering thought. You can quit whenever you wish to. If the weather suddenly turns bad, you can go back. You are not a quitter! You are just making judicious decisions!

So, learn more about yourself as well as the trail. Challenge yourself and just take a hike! You'll be glad you did.

CHAPTER 8

Recipes for the Couch Potato

FOOD IS AN IMPORTANT PART of any experience. Food you take on a hike should not be perishable or need a lot of preparation. After all, we're Couch Potatoes—we don't want to work that hard, right? You should also like what you take. If you have food allergies, check to make sure that trail food does not include the things that you cannot tolerate.

Note: For ease of preparation, recipes with many ingredients have a list. If the recipes are really simple, the ingredients are just **bolded**.

Important to all hikers is trail mix or "gorp"— ("good ol' raisins and peanuts"). It can be easily packed, conveniently eaten, and doesn't need to have refrigeration or special handling.

The Hiking Couch Potato Easy Trail Mix

Use one cup of whichever of the following items you like. Plan to mix the ingredients and take a cup or two in a sealed plastic bag. This can be stored easily in one of the multitude of pockets you will have.

Items for trail mix:

Raisins	Nuts—any variety you prefer or one type only
Sunflower seeds	Pumpkin seeds
Sesame sticks	Other dried fruit
Small pretzels	Chocolate chips (not in warm weather)

Add salt or any flavoring you prefer such as adobo, lemon salt, etc. If you have high blood pressure, skip the salt. This versatile recipe can make enough for a group and can be varied to appeal to anyone.

Jerky

If you're looking for a protein fix, one of the jerkies— they're made in many varieties and flavors—might be a good option for you. They take a long time to chew—a very long time. We never finished the giant economy size bag we bought. See, the easiest recipe of all: go to store, buy a bag.

Messier (but Great) Stuff for a Trail
Peanut Butter and Celery

Spread **peanut butter** in **celery** segments that are cut in 3-inch sections. Put two pieces together with the peanut butter portions facing each other. Wrap each two-section bundle tightly. Put several of these bundles in a small, plastic sealed bag with a cold pack or ice cubes (sealed also, separately) to keep them cool. When the ice melts, you can drink that, too.

Peanut butter is a great protein pick-me-up: Unless you're allergic. In which case, do not bring this recipe.

Popcorn

Popcorn can be wonderful, but it can stick in your teeth and be annoying. Dentists hate popcorn. If you love the stuff, sprinkle freshly made **popcorn** (we prefer the hot air variety) with **parmesan or romano** cheese. Bring it in the ubiquitous sealed plastic bag.

Andrew's Favorite Snack

This is easy to make, but can be a messy treat. It is refreshing, crunchy and a good protein source.

Take **one apple** per person. Core the apple with a knife or peeler, making sure you have removed the seeds and the tough inner core. Fill the opening with **peanut butter** (your choice, smooth or crunchy). Save in a plastic bag, one per bag. Enjoy!

Oatmeal Cookies

The Couch Potato loves oatmeal cookies with raisins. Her hiking partner (translate husband) hates raisins. This can necessitate the great compromise of the decade. You can do without raisins; or make two batches, one with and one without. You can buy them in the store and save all the fussing. You choose! This is the recipe the Couch Potato follows when she's feeling ambitious and wants to make oatmeal cookies. (And her husband picks out the raisins in his cookies, so we're both happy.)

Preheat oven to 375° F.

Ingredients:

½ cup butter	¾ cups brown sugar
¼ granulated sugar	1 egg
½ teaspoon vanilla extract	½ teaspoon baking soda
½ teaspoon salt	1½ cups oats (quick cooking variety)

1 cup of wheat flour (or substitute *part* of this with another flour such as spelt, or wheat germ, rice flour, etc.)

½ cup of raisins

Add any of the following that you have and like:
> Nuts—chopped—walnut, pecan preferred—½ cup
> Small chocolate drops—½ cup
> Flaked coconut—¼ cup
> Crunchy rice cereal—½ cup
> Milk—optional —small amount to moisten just
>   a little

1. Cream butter and sugars until light and smooth.
2. Beat in eggs and vanilla.
3. Blend dry ingredients: flour, salt, baking soda. Add to the above.
4. Stir in oats, raisins and other ingredients. If it is a little thick and hard to stir, that is okay. If it is extremely hard to mix because you've emptied the extra ingredients from your pantry suggested in the list above, add a few drops of milk to make it move. You don't want a very wet consistency. It should be like mortar, not like toothpaste.
5. Form into balls from 1–3 inches across. Put on a cookie sheet and flatten each ball slightly.
6. Bake for 12 minutes or until the cookies are slightly browned, but not burned. Remove from baking sheet and cool.

Bring along in sealed plastic bags. Enjoy!

Potato Recipes for the Couch Potato

Seriously, as a Couch Potato, how could we not include some recipes that include potatoes?

With no real calories beyond the potato itself, potatoes contain potassium, fiber, calcium, vitamins A, C, and B6, iron, protein, and many other great nutrients. This has *not* been a paid endorsement. We *really* like potatoes. Eaten in moderation without all of the fattening toppings, potatoes are a terrific food. Potato councils rejoice! If you are following one of the low carb diets, eating part of a potato once in a while will keep the joy in life.

The following recipes would be eaten at home, since they are better warm and tend to be messy. It would be a little difficult to take them on the trail!

Unfried Fries

This easy recipe for unfried French fries uses no real oil or fats. The trick is the non-stick spray!

Preheat the oven to 450° F.

1. Take *one potato per person* and cut into 8 wedges. (Cut in half the long way, then cut each half into 4 pieces.)
2. Take a large cookie sheet or low-edged baking pan and spray with **non-stick spray**.

3. Place the potato wedges on the tray and spray them with the *non-stick spray*. Do not overlap the fries. Flavored non-stick sprays such as an olive oil spray are especially good.

4. Sprinkle the "fries" with any **seasoning** you like—a spicy Cajun or chili mix would add real zing. You can try salt and pepper or anything you prefer.

5. Place the tray in the oven and let bake for a total of 20–25 minutes, turning at least once to get all sides. Check after it has baked to see if it is crispy enough for your liking. Since every potato is different, as well as every oven, this is an individual preference. You can make the oven a little hotter, too.

6. Remove and cool slightly so no one burns their mouth. Eat and enjoy.

The following savory-sweet recipe uses sweet potatoes. When the Couch Potato made it for Thanksgiving dinner, it was so good that everyone wanted more, so she made a second batch. (Published by permission of Worldwide Recipes *www.worldwiderecipes.com*)

Apple, Leek, and Sweet Potato Gratin

1¼ cups (310 ml) heavy cream

2 large leeks, thinly sliced with first ½" of fuzzy root end removed, thoroughly rinsed, using only the white part and first inch of the light green part. (Leeks tend to be sandy, so separate slices and really rinse well.)

2 Tbs (30 ml) chopped fresh thyme, or 2 tsp (10 ml) dried

Salt and freshly ground pepper to taste

A grating of fresh nutmeg

2 large sweet potatoes (about 1 lb, 450 g), peeled and thinly sliced

2 cups (500 ml) grated cheddar cheese

1 large apple, cored and thinly sliced

1. Combine the cream, leeks, thyme, salt, pepper, and nutmeg in a saucepan and bring to a boil over moderate heat, stirring occasionally.
2. Add the sweet potatoes, cover and simmer 10 minutes.
3. Layer half the sweet potato mixture in a buttered baking dish.
4. Top with the sliced apple.
5. Repeat with sweet potato mixture and cheese.
6. Bake uncovered in a preheated 375° F (190° C) oven for about 45 minutes, until bubbling and golden brown. Serves 6 to 8.

Shepherd-Less Pie

This is a recipe the Couch Potato has made many times, which she varies every time she makes it. It's a hearty recipe that fills you up and is very flavorful. It is also great as a vegetarian entree.

Ingredients:

> 2 – 16 oz. cans of beans (great northern, cannellini, white pea beans, etc.), drained
> 1 carrot—chopped
> 3 large potatoes—cut in quarters
> 1 stalk of celery—chopped
> 2 garlic cloves—chopped
> 1 medium onion or 3 scallions
> 2½ cups vegetable bouillon
> 4 mushrooms—any variety, chopped
> ¼ cup TVP chunks (textured vegetable protein—available at health food stores and some large supermarkets)
> 1½ tsp.–2 tsps.—thyme, parsley, salt, pepper, and/or any dried herbs you like
> Bay leaf
> Topping—¼ cup of bread crumbs, nuts or wheat germ

1. Boil 3 large potatoes covered in water in their skins until tender (about 15–20 minutes.) If salt is not a problem for you, add a little to the cooking

water. Reserve some of the water (maybe a cup) from the cooking.

2. Peel and mash the 3 potatoes, seasoning with salt, pepper and a light sprinkling of the herbs, using a bit of the water that the potato was boiled in to make the mashed potatoes smooth, but not runny. This should be a very thick consistency.

3. Fry the onions, celery, carrot, garlic until the onion is just starting to brown slightly.

4. Add the mushrooms and beans to the cooking onion mixture and cook for about 2 minutes.

5. Add the bay leaves, bouillon, remainder of the herbs, and TVP.

6. Simmer for 10 minutes.

7. Put the cooked mixture in an ovenproof casserole, removing the bay leaf.

8. Spread the mashed potatoes on the top of the vegetable mixture, covering it completely.

9. Sprinkle bread crumbs, nuts or wheat germ over the mashed potatoes.

10. Broil until top is lightly browned.

11. Scoop, serving with potato showing on top. This recipe can also be made in individual ramekins to serve each person their own "pie."

Note: This may be reheated and tastes even better the next day when the flavors have had the chance to soak in.

CHAPTER 9

Final Thoughts on Hiking and the Challenges of Life

YES, INDEED, THIS IS the Couch Potato's final attempt to provide pithy and motivating thoughts, one more set of reasons to get up from the couch.

The philosopher, Rene Descartes, claimed, "I think, therefore I am." Much like the child's book about the *Little Engine That Could* (Penguin Putnam), know that if you think you can, *you can*. Know that beyond just thinking and being, there is so much you can accomplish. When people offer the half-full glass, opt for the *completely* full one! Nothing else will do!

You can have your couch as well as a fulfilling outdoor adventure that will remind you of your place in the world. Remember, the couch will still be there when you get home. (Unless, of course, your couch has been stolen while you were out hiking. Do remember to lock your door before you leave your home to go hiking.) However, the experiences you have will enrich every aspect of your life—even while on the couch. When you watch television and see a running sequence—typically when the star is chasing the "bad guy"—that goes on and on and on, you can comment that they can't be in such good shape! No one could run as long as that without breaking a sweat!

So, having a realistic sense of what your body can accomplish is vital. With all of the hiking, the Couch Potato has never had an injury. Recently, she pulled her bike out of mothballs and scraped up her knee the first week back on the bike. She thinks she will go back to hiking—both feet are never off the ground at one time and balance is not something to worry about when hiking. Also, hikers tend to be a polite bunch. They get out of the way for oncoming traffic!

(Confirmed bicyclists can comment for my upcoming book, *Biking for the Couch Potato*.)

And remember, don't overdo it! Slowly build the time and difficulty of the hikes you attempt. If your

feet hurt, soak them! (Seriously, a pan of warm water with Epsom salts can do wonders.)

We look forward to seeing you out on the trail—(with your hiking partner or group!).

Coming soon: Other Couch Potato books and related "stuff" to remind you that it is time to get up, get out and get moving! Meanwhile, see *http://hiking. forthecouchpotato.com* for new Couch Potato items as they become available—and we don't mean butter, sour cream, and bacon bits!

Also, on the Web site, we'll be organizing Couch Potato hiking groups, so people can share the experience! Motivation is easier with many people!

Hikes Mentioned in this Book

THESE ARE OFFERED IN the order we listed them in Chapter 6. We provide as much information as possible without being "A Guide Book of Hiking Trails for the Couch Potato." Links are offered for anyone looking for more information from the direct sources. Hikes shown are examples of places where we have enjoyed easy hiking, and are not intended to be an exhaustive list. For that, the Couch Potato would be too exhausted to actually get out and do the hiking!

Recommendations for additional hikes are welcomed from our hiking Couch Potato community and can be submitted to: *http://hiking.forthecouchpotato.com*

Massachusetts
Massachusetts State Parks
http://www.mass.gov/dcr/forparks.htm

Freedom Trail
www.thefreedomtrail.org

LOCATION: Boston, Massachusetts. 2.5 miles thru Beacon Hill, Downtown Boston, the North End and Charlestown

ACCESSIBILITY: Most of the trail is quite accessible, but sites like Bunker Hill Monument, with almost 300 steps, are not accessible. (They are difficult, narrow, wedge-shaped steps-even tough for someone able to walk.) The Freedom Trail is self-guided, so go at your own pace. Guided tours and trolleys are available for a fee. If you decide to walk the Trail in its entirety, plan a full day—or more—if you are going to stop at sights along the Trail.

ADMISSION: The Trail itself has no fee, but sites along the way can have fees. Paul Revere's Home, for instance, charges: Adults: $3.00, Seniors and College Students: $2.50, Children (ages 5–17): $1.00. Old South

Meeting House and Old State House also charge fees. Everything else is free.

HOURS: Vary at historic locations, but you can walk the physical trail anytime.

The Freedom Trail offers many sights and can be entered at numerous points to see historic and scenic vistas in Boston. (See description in Chapter 6.) One especially fun place to stop for restaurants, entertainment and tourist goodies is Faneuil Hall and its vicinity. The National Parks Service offers free historical tours on the half-hour from 9:30 AM–4:30 PM.

Another historical site of especial interest to history buffs is "Old Ironsides"—the "USS Constitution … (which) is the oldest commissioned warship afloat in the world." Guided tours and self tours are also free.

Washington, D.C. and Maryland
Washington, D.C. Parks Department
http://dpr.dc.gov/DC/DPR

Maryland Department of Natural Resources
(Park locator)
http://www.dnr.state.md.us/publiclands/mdmap.asp

C & O (Chesapeake and Ohio) Canal National Historic Park, Washington, D.C. and Maryland
http://www.nps.gov/choh

LOCATION: THE C & O CANAL meanders 184.5 miles from Cumberland, Maryland on the north to Georgetown in Washington, D. C. on the south, following the path of the original canal that was the commercial lifeline for the Potomac River area. There are six visitor centers along the canal with hours differing, depending on the season.

ACCESSIBLIITY: Some trail areas are uneven, but the National Parks Department tries to make visitor centers and some areas accessible. There are walkways and the mule-drawn canal boats can be boarded by people with some mobility.

ADMISSION: A three-day pass is $5 for a private vehicle or $3 per person for those who walk or bike in. An annual National Historic Park pass or Maryland Annual Park Pass is $20. Canal boat fees are $5 per person age 4 and over.

HOURS: Daylight hours. Visitor center hours may vary. Check the Web site for the location you prefer. More services are offered in spring, summer, and fall.

The C & O Canal NHP is a wonderland of natural and historic activities. Take a canal ride and let the mules do the work or hike on one of the trail segments that skirt the canal. (As a hiker, do spend some time hiking!) Great Falls is a must-see scenic view if you are in the area. You can follow walkways that provide a great view and some exercise.

The visitor centers, as well as the historic interpreters on the boats, give visitors a sense of what it was like two hundred years ago. There are so many miles of trail that, if you are visiting or live in the vicinity, you would not run out of places to explore.

Virginia
Virginia State Parks
http://www.dcr.state.va.us/parks/index.htm

Waller Mill Park–City Of Williamsburg, Virginia
http://www.williamsburgva.gov/Index.aspx?page=477

LOCATION: Airport Road (Rt. 645) between I-64 and Rt. 60 West

ACCESSIBILITY: The main paved path is accessible to strollers and wheelchairs, although the varied hilly terrain will demand some exertion.

ADMISSION: $2.00 per vehicle

HOURS: Sunrise to Sunset—varies by season

A 2,700-acre park surrounding a 286-acre lake/ reservoir that was created during WWII for the adjacent Camp Peary, which is available for fishing, boating, pedal boating, and canoeing. A tunnel connects the upper and lower sections of the lake.

There are currently two hiking trails:

The **Bayberry Nature Trail** is a .92 mile loop. A self-guided trail booklet is available at the park headquarters located near the boathouse.

The **Lookout Tower Trail** is a 2.92 mile loop passing an observation tower with views of the reservoir.

Rockwood Park–Richmond, Virginia (Chesterfield County)

http://www.chesterfield.gov/content2.aspx?id=5921&ek mensel=c580fa7b_252_253_5921_18

LOCATION: 3401 Courthouse Road

DIRECTIONS: From Richmond: Take Hull Street (Route 360) West from Chippenham Parkway 4.4 miles to Courthouse Rd. Turn right on Courthouse Rd. Park entrance is *only* on your right.

ACCESSIBILITY: The main paved path is accessible to strollers and wheelchairs, although the varied hilly terrain will demand some exertion.

ADMISSION: Free (There is a fee for picnic facility reservations.)

HOURS: Not listed

A 163-acre park featuring a complex of ball fields, tennis courts, a nature center, a multi-station archery range, garden plots and an extensive system of trails. The trails are all suitable for Couch Potatoes, being only 1.5 miles or less. Although a paved path circles the park, there are many dirt paths that lead off of the main path, several skirting the border of Gregory's Pond. *Note:* The Adobe map online does not differentiate between paved and dirt trails.

Minnesota
Minnesota State Parks
http://www.dnr.state.mn.us/state_parks/index.html

Minnesota State Trails
http://www.dnr.state.mn.us/state_trails/index.html

Check this out! Very helpful and they even offer virtual tours of trails.

Como Park
http://www.comozooconservatory.org/como_park/ index.shtml

LOCATION: St. Paul, Minnesota, 1360 North Lexington Parkway, in the Como Park neighborhood

ACCESSIBLITY: Accessible. "Visitors with limited mobility are encouraged to use the historic entrance of the Marjorie McNeely Conservatory on Fridays,

Saturdays, Sundays and Holidays." Visitors with accessibility needs on other days should call the "Visitor Services Office (651-487-8201) ahead of your visit to arrange to have a Como staff person waiting to admit you at the historic entrance."

ADMISSION: A donation of $2 for adults and $1 for children is requested (not required) for entrance to the zoo and conservatory, but walking the grounds is free.

HOURS: Walking the grounds at any time is possible. To visit the conservatory and zoo, hours are: 10 AM to 4 PM from October to March; and 10 AM to 6 PM from April to September.

Como Park offers a zoo and conservatory, but there are trails that circle the park and provide some gently curving ups and downs. The zoo offers lions and tigers and bears … oh, my (a nod to *The Wizard of Oz* and Dorothy) plus monkeys, giraffes, sea lions, and other land and aquatic animals. In season, there is a delightful antique carousel for the young and young-at-heart. (Fee—$1.50 per ride.)

The conservatory has some gorgeous indoor and outdoor gardens. The indoor displays are housed in a unique giant greenhouse.

(Note to those taking our effort to encourage hiking very seriously: If you briskly walk the grounds of

Como Park, that qualifies as a hike. While strolling the grounds does not qualify as a "hike," at least you're up and moving about, taking in interesting sights, and stimulating your mind and body at the same time.)

Arizona
Arizona State Parks
www.pr.state.az.us

South Mountain Park
www.phoenix.gov/PARKS/hikesoth.html

LOCATION: South of Baseline Rd. and west of Interstate 10 in the City of Phoenix

DIRECTIONS: To South Mountain Park (Main Entrance)

> From I-17 going south: exit 7th Ave./Central Ave. Stay on Frontage Road to Central, turn right to go south.
> From I-10 going east: exit 7th Ave. Go south to Baseline Road, east on Baseline to Central Ave., turn right to go south on Central Ave.
> From I-10 going west: exit Baseline Road, turn left, go to Central Ave. and turn left (south).

ACCESSIBILITY: Although some trails are flat, this is not an easy park for accessibility. Trails are uneven.

ADMISSION: In August, 2010, the City of Phoenix instituted a first-time fee for parking at some of their parks. The Pima Canyon trailhead at South Mountain Park will have a $2 daily parking fee or a $50 six-month parking pass. Walking or biking in or using other trailhead areas of the park will not require a fee. For more information, see *http://phoenix.gov/PRL/passupdate.html*

HOURS: 5 AM to 7 PM (Facilities). Trails remain open until 11 PM

South Mountain Park holds the distinction of being the largest city park in the United States at over 16,000 acres. The park features over fifty-eight miles of trails for hiking, biking and horseback riding for all ability levels.

At 2,330 feet, Dobbins Lookout is the highest point in the park accessible by trail.

If you have an hour or all day to hike, there are trails ranging from one to fourteen miles.

The trail lengths shown on the Park's map and listed below appear to be one way only. Allow time and resources accordingly. The trails below are arranged by length of hike. Kiwanis is a favorite of the Couch Potato's because of the view of Phoenix, but it does get steep at the end. (A hiking map and trail guide are available online.)

Kiwanis Trail
Length: 1.0 mile
Difficulty: Moderate—steep toward the top end.

Mormon Trail
Length: 1.1 miles
Difficulty: Moderate to difficult (elevation change of about 1,000 feet)

Ranger Trail
Length: 1.4 mile, one way
Difficulty: Moderate—steep switchbacks toward the top end

Beverly Canyon Trail
Length: 1.5 miles
Difficulty: Moderate—some short, steep sections

Telegraph Pass Trail
Length: 1.5 miles to Telegraph Pass. First 0.5 mile is paved.
Difficulty: Easy to moderate—steep sections toward the top

Javelina Canyon Trail
Length: 1.7 miles
Difficulty: Easy to moderate

Bajada Trail
Length: 2 miles
Difficulty: Easy to moderate

Pima Canyon–Pima Gulch
Length: 2.2 miles
Difficulty: Moderate

Holbert Trail
Length: 2.5 miles
Difficulty: Difficult—fairly steep and long

Alta Trail
Length: 4.5 miles
Difficulty: Very difficult—very steep on both ends

Desert Classic Trail
Length: 9 miles
Difficulty: Moderate to difficult—mainly due to the length

National Trail
Length: 14.3 miles
Difficulty: Moderate to difficult

Utah
Utah State Parks
www.stateparks.utah.gov

Zion National Park
www.nps.gov/zion

LOCATION: Springdale, Utah

ACCESSIBILITY: From April to October, entrance into the park is by accessible shuttle buses only. Much of the ground is uneven, so accessibility varies. Pa'rus Trail and Riverside Walk are paved.

ADMISSION: $25.00 National Park Fee

HOURS: Zion Visitor Center opens daily at 8 AM, with closings from 5 PM to 8 PM, depending on the season. Trails are open with no specific closure hours.

TRAILS: Breathtaking views greet you on the trails. Zion has soaring cliffs, wildlife and water features that provide excellent photographic opportunities. Hiking times given are suggested by the park, but could vary depending on your speed and how often you stop to observe.

Pa'rus Trail

3.5 miles

1.5 hours

Easy—Paved trail follows Virgin River from south campground

Weeping Rock

.5 miles

30 minutes

Short/Steep—Minor drop-offs. Paved trail to rack alcove with dripping springs.

Riverside Walk

2 miles

1.5 hours

Easy—Minor drop-offs. Paved trail along Virgin River at bottom of narrow canyon

Emerald Pools Trails

Lower Emerald Pool Trail

.6 miles, one way

69-foot ascent

Easy—Paved trail to pool and behind the waterfalls

California
California State Parks
www.parks.ca.gov

Muir Woods
www.nps.gov/muwo

LOCATION/DIRECTIONS: North of the Golden Gate Bridge on the highway. Take Highway 1 exit and follow the signs at each intersection directing you to Muir Woods.

ACCESSIBILITY: 1.5 miles of flat paved trails are accessible to strollers, and wheelchairs

ADMISSION: $5.00 National Park Fee

HOURS: 8 AM to sunset, including holidays

Muir Woods National Monument became the 7th National Monument in the US in 1908. For an extremely busy park, there is limited parking near the gate. Don't be surprised if you have to park up to a mile away during the summer and weekends. You might want to arrive early or wait until later in the afternoon.

There are six miles of trails and fire roads in the park that connect with others in the surrounding area. There are also three loop trails that range from a half hour to one and one-half hours. (A trail map is available by clicking on the highlighted word "trails" on the "Things To Do" page of the NPS website noted below.)

(We suggest you scroll down the left side of the page and click on *"Plan Your Visit"* & *"Frequently Asked Questions" [FAQs].)*

National Park Service
http://www.nps.gov

Resource Directory

Calorie Calculator

See *http://www.healthyweightforum.org/* for an easy-to-use calorie calculator that lets you enter your weight, the activity, the amount of time you're spending—and voila! You have the number of calories you're likely burning from that activity.

Outdoor Products Retailers:

Altrec
http://www.altrec.com

Bass Pro Shops
www.basspro.com

Blueridge Mountain Sports
www.brmsstore.com

Cabela's
www.cabelas.com

Campmor
www.campmor.com

Columbia Sportswear
www.columbia.com

Eastern Mountain Sports
www.ems.com

LL Bean
www.llbean.com

REI
www.rei.com

(*Note:* REI is a consumer cooperative—Once you've joined, you are a member for life.)

Sierra Trading Post
www.sierratradingpost.com

HIKING POLES:
Black Diamond
http://www.blackdiamondequipment.com/en-us/shop/mountain/trekking-poles

Leki
www.leki.com

HYDRATION SYSTEMS:
Camelbak
www.camelbak.com

Deuter
www.deuterusa.com

High Sierra Sports
http://highsierrasport.com/

SOCKS:
Dahlgren
www.dahlgrenfootwear.com

Thorlo
http://www.thorlo.com/hiking-socks.php

Smartwool
www.smartwool.com

HIKING SHOES/BOOTS: (DAY HIKING)

Asolo
www.asolo.com

Columbia
www.columbia.com

Danner
www.danner.com

Garmont
www.garmont.com

Lowa
www.lowaboots.com

Merrell
www.merrell.com

Montrail
www.montrail.com

Sportiva
www.sportiva.com

Timberland
www.timberland.com

Vasque
www.vasque.com

Let's Talk Taters

Potato History

At this time, there are more than 160 potato species with more being developed yearly. The first to be deemed edible were cultivated at least 2,000 years ago in the mountains of Peru.

Potatoes were introduced into European culture around the 1570s in Spain. They literally hit English soil about 1590. Those first potatoes in Spain were used as medicine grown almost exclusively by pharmacists. The large-scale cultivation that we know today didn't begin until the nineteenth century.

French Fries–Are They Really from France?

Actually, yes! Or maybe not … according to the people of Belgium. In the 1840s, pommes frites, (fried potatoes in English) appeared in Paris—or was it Belgium? The jury's still out!

Although it is not known which chef first created pommes frites, they became popular almost overnight. Pushcart vendors in Paris streets sold them much like the famous hot dog vendors of New York City. In Belgium, pommes frites are considered a treasure of national proportions, where they are still prepared from fresh potatoes and sold on the streets from numerous french-fry shacks, known as fritures or frietkoets.

Pommes frites spread to the American colonies where they were called "French fried potatoes" (go figure!). The name was shortened to "French fries" in the 1930s. (Maybe someday there will be a high level secret meeting to change the name to "Belgian fries.")

In 1864, Britain's French fried potatoes ("chips") fell into a basket with fried fish to become the extremely popular fish and chips.

Although French fries are eaten with ketchup in the US, malt vinegar in England, and with mayonnaise in the Netherlands, the French, for the most part, eat them without any condiments.

Potato Chips ... Saratoga Chips ...

American as, well, potato chips!

Saratoga, New York gets the nod for the chip. They were even called "Saratoga Chips" until the 1920s. A resort chef was noted to have sliced a potato extremely thin after an annoying patron sent his "too thick" French Fries back to the kitchen. The old adage "don't make the chef mad" actually backfired.

The patron was actually extremely happy about the thin, fried potato and the Saratoga Chip was born.

What's a Spud?

Although the history of the term is cloaked in a wee bit of mystery, the slang "spud" probably found its way into our language due to the spade-like tool used to dig them out of the ground.

So, You Want More Information about Potatoes?

We've got web links about your Big Potatoes, your little potatoes, your spuds, your tubers, your health, your state commissions, and even your potato festivals ...

Is this an exhaustive list? You bet your spuds it's not! But hey, this is a short book.

Potato Crop Production by State–2010

(Compiled by the USDA)

*http://usda.mannlib.cornell.edu/MannUsda/
viewDocumentoInfo.do?documentID=1046*

1. Idaho
2. Washington
3. North Dakota
4. Wisconsin
5. Colorado
6. Maine
7. Michigan
8. Minnesota
9. Oregon
10. Nebraska

Canadian Potato Crop Production
by Province–2009

(Statistics Canada—Agriculture Division—
Canadian Potato Production Bulletin)

*http://www.statcan.gc.ca/pub/22-008-x/
22-008-x2010001-eng.pdf*

1. Prince Edward Island
2. Manitoba
3. New Brunswick
4. Alberta
5. Quebec
6. Ontario

7. Saskatchewan
8. British Columbia
9. Nova Scotia
10. Newfoundland and Labrador

What's a Tuber?

Unlike many other vegetables, potatoes do not have roots. Their stems are known as "tubers." It takes a soil temperature between 60° and 70°F. to grow a potato. If the soil temperature goes above 80°F., call it a day and find another crop to grow. Even though it is possible to grow potatoes in just about any state in the country during cool times of the year, it's the northern states that get the "maximum yield," as they say in the business.

That's why our list of the top ten potato growing states doesn't include Arizona and Florida!

Potato Types

Potatoes may well be the most popular vegetable in the United States. But, it is estimated that out of the over 100 varieties, only about six are used commercially.

The variety known as "Russet Burbank" is the most widely grown commercial variety of potato produced in the United States. As potato varieties are seasonal in their growth patterns, potatoes can be available year-round. It is also one of only a few crops that can be stored under conditions that make them ready for processing and shipping at any time.

Potatoes can be baked, boiled, fried, mashed, and steamed, making it one of the most versatile vegetables. While some cooks prefer certain varieties for a particular purpose, the new Klondike Rose™ variety is adaptable to most preparation methods.

Light Brown Skin

Allegany	Atlantic	CalWhite
Cascade	Castile	Chipeta
Gemchip	Irish Cobbler	Itasca
Kanona	Katahdin	Kennebec
La Chipper	Monona	Norchip
Norwis	Onaway	Ontario
Pike	Sebago	Shepody
Snowden	Superior	White Rose
Yukon Gold		

Red Skin

Chieftain	Klondike Rose™	La Rouge
NorDonna	Norland	Red La Soda
Red Pontiac	Red Ruby	Sangre
Viking		

Dark Brown Skin

BelRus	Centennial Russet	Century Russet
Frontier Russet	Goldrush	Hilite Russet
Krantz	Lemhi Russet	Nooksack
Norgold Russet	Norking Russet	Ranger Russet
Russet Burbank	Russet Norkotah	Russet Nugget

Nutrition Facts*
(1 oblong white, baked, about 2" x 4¾")

Calories 145

Protein 3.06 grams

Carbohydrates 33.63 grams

Dietary Fiber 2.34 grams

Calcium 7.80 mg

Iron .55 mg

Magnesium 39.00 mg

Potassium 609.96 mg

Phosphorus 78.00 mg

Vitamin C 19.97 mg

Niacin 2.17 mg

Folate 14.20 mcg

*Nutrition facts courtesy of University of Illinois Extension
http://urbanext.illinois.edu/veggies/potato.cfm

But aren't potatoes high in carbohydrates? Yes, but the potato has so many other good qualities as a source for many vitamins and minerals that you can forgive the carb count. If you are looking for fiber and just about every vitamin and mineral except vitamin A, it's a great choice.

Potatoes are fat-free and cholesterol-free. Potatoes are also high in vitamin C and a good source of potassium.

And, best of all, potatoes taste great and are relatively low in calories, unless you decide to pile on the butter … sour cream … bacon bits …! (You know them as the "Fully-Loaded Potato" at your local restaurant. If you must, ask for your favorite toppings "on the side." Used sparingly, the toppings won't contribute as much to those unhealthy conditions we are trying to avoid by hiking.)

Consumer Sites

POTANDON PRODUCE
http://www.potandon.com
http://www.klondikebrands.com/
The largest seller of fresh potatoes in the US, Potandon's Web site has recipes, details on potato varieties and other potato-related information. They are the sole US providers of the new Klondike Rose™* potato that has a red skin, but the inner qualities of a gold-fleshed

potato. This newly developed variety can be mashed, baked, grilled and you name it!

(Klondike Rose™ is a registered trademark of Sunrain Varieties LLC, used under license by Potandon Produce LLC ©2010 Sunrain.)

THE HEALTHY POTATO
www.healthypotato.com

The United States Potato Board (USPB) was established in 1971 by a group of potato growers to promote the benefits of eating potatoes. Headquartered in Denver, Colorado, the USPB represents more than 3,000 potato growers and handlers across the country.

Through consumer public relations, nutrition education, retail programs, foodservice marketing and export programs, the USPB strives to educate consumers, retailers and culinary professionals about the convenience, great nutritional value and versatility of potatoes.

State Commissions

Idaho Potato Commission
www.famouspotatoes.com

Washington State Potato Commission
http://www.potatoes.com

Wisconsin Potato & Vegetable Growers Association
http://www.wisconsinpotatoes.com

Colorado Potato Administrative Committee
www.coloradopotato.org

The Oregon Potato Commission
www.oregonspuds.com

The Maine Potato Board
www.mainepotatoes.com

Michigan Potato Industry Commission
www.mipotato.com

Empire State Potato Growers Inc. (New York)
www.empirepotatogrowers.com*

* Turn up the volume on your computer and *sing along* to the "New York State Potato Song" …

Canadian Provincial Commissions

Prince Edward Island
www.peipotato.org/

Manitoba
www.gov.mb.ca/agriculture/crops/potatoes/

Alberta
http://www.albertapotatoes.ca/

New Brunswick
http://www.potatoesnb.com/

And for the Tourists ...
The Potato Museum ... Yes! ... No Kidding!

Idaho Potato Museum
http://www.potatoexpo.com/
Blackfoot, Idaho

Admission:
Per person: Adults—$3.00, Seniors/AAA members—$2.50, Children (6–12)—$1.00; under 6—free

Groups: 15 or more—$2.00 each

There is an amazing amount of history and potato memorabilia crammed into this museum with a gift shop for souvenirs. And, everyone who visits gets a free potato sample!

Hours: April–September: 9:30 AM–5:00 PM, Monday–Saturday
October–March: 9:30 AM–3:00 PM, Monday–Friday

They are closed on major holidays and for the week from Christmas through New Year's.

And, guess what ... there is another!

The Potato Museum
http://www.peipotatomuseum.com

O'Leary, Prince Edward Island, Canada

Admission:
Per person: $6.00 plus 7% GST (Goods and Services Tax)
Per family (parents and children): $14.00 plus 7% GST

Hours: Monday–Saturday: 9 AM to 5 PM
Sunday: 1 PM to 5 PM

Open: May 15 to October 1

US Potato Festivals
Yes, siree! That's what we said! Potato Festivals!

Now you would think that we're talking the big city here. Boise, Portland, Minneapolis.

Not on your spuds we're not!

We're talking *real* potato towns!

Barnesville! Fort Fairfield! O'Leary! Shelley!

Wait a minute! Isn't that last one the name of our author? That's just toooo weird! (The Couch Potato has recently visited Shelley, a charming small town.)

The following are the most famous festivals we could find. Some are two days and others are up to ten days!

So here they are …

Potato Blossom Festival
Mid-July
Fort Fairfield, Maine, Pop. 4011
Over 60 years and counting!
www.potatoblossom.org

Potato Days Festival
Late August
Barnesville, Minnesota, Pop. 2173
Celebrating for over 70-plus years
www.potatodays.com

Annual Idaho Spud Day
Mid-September
Shelley, Idaho, Pop. 3813
www.ci.shelley.id.us
Go to "Events" tab

Canadian Potato Festivals

Potato Blossom Festival
Late July
O'Leary, Prince Edward Island, Pop. 877
Annual Event—over 40 years
http://www.exhibitions-festivalspeiae.com/peipotato blossomfestival.html

Alliston Potato Festival

Early August
Alliston, Ontario, Pop. Approx. 9679
Annual Event—for almost 40 years!
http://www.allistonpotatofestival.com/

Finally:

Keep up with the Couch Potato by checking out our Web site:

http://hiking.forthecouchpotato.com

Coming soon: Future "for the Couch Potato" books and other Couch Potato "stuff," but not stuffed potatoes.

Join the Couch Potato community by submitting ideas for hikes, letting other Couch Potatoes know when you hike so they can applaud you, sharing recipes, and helping form Couch Potato Hiking Clubs.

Get up and get going! See you on the trail!

Andrew's Favorite
    Snack, 71–2
Apple, Leek, and
    Sweet Potato Gratin,
    76
Hiking Couch Potato
    Easy Trail Mix, 70
jerky, 70–1
oatmeal cookies, 72–3
peanut butter and
    celery, 71
popcorn, 71
Shepherd-less Pie, 77–8
Unfried Fries, 74–5
researching hikes, 32
resource directory, 99–103
resting, adequate, 39–40
restrooms, trail, 36–7
Rockwood Park (Virginia),
    40, 54–5, 88–9

safety
    hiking alone and, 34,
        40
    hydration and, 29
    lightning and, 30
    physical condition
        and, 30
    rain and, 29–30
Saratoga Chips, 107
self-expression, hiking
    and, 43
self-knowledge, hiking
    and, 36, 38–9

Shepherd-less Pie, 77–8
shoes, hiking
    choosing, 19–20
    resources for, 102–3
socks, hiking
    choosing, 21
    resources for, 101
South Mountain Park
    (Phoenix, AZ), 56, 91–4
"spud," origin of, 107
stamina, 39–41
sticks, hiking, 22
sunburn, avoiding, 24
sunscreen, choice of, 24

toilet paper, 36
trail maps, 33–4
tubers, 109. *See also*
    potatoes.

Unfried Fries, 74–5
United States Potato
    Board, 113
urban setting, hiking in, 7,
    32, 38
Utah, hike in, 95–6

Virginia, hikes in, 87–9

walking, hiking vs., 4, 14,
    38, 43–5
Waller Mill Park
    (Virginia), 53–4, 87–8

.

ABOUT THE AUTHOR

FORMERLY A CONFIRMED COUCH POTATO, Shelley Gillespie became a hiker due to her husband's insistence. Then, she discovered she actually liked hiking! The Gillespies have since hiked or walked on both US coasts and in many other scenic locations.

A journalist and public relations consultant, she lives in Arizona where hiking in the summer can sometimes be accomplished in an air-conditioned, two-story shopping mall or outside early in the morning before temperatures exceed 100+ degrees.

When not writing or hiking, Shelley is cooking for friends and family, and volunteering in her community.

Visit her Web site at *FortheCouchPotato.com*